THE BROKEN
Bride

REDEFINING THE CHURCH

Loni M. Stankan

WESTBOW
PRESS®
A DIVISION OF THOMAS NELSON
& ZONDERVAN

WestBow Press books may be ordered through booksellers or by contacting:

WestBow Press
A Division of Thomas Nelson & Zondervan
1663 Liberty Drive
Bloomington, IN 47403
www.westbowpress.com
844-714-3454

ISBN: 978-1-6642-9030-3 (sc)
ISBN: 978-1-6642-9029-7 (hc)
ISBN: 978-1-6642-9031-0 (e)

Library of Congress Control Number: 2023901217

Print information available on the last page.

WestBow Press rev. date: 01/26/2023

I cannot move forward with submitting this manuscript until I take the time to thank a few people for their endless support, love, and encouragement as I fulfilled a desire that has been on my heart since I first picked up a pen and piece of paper. Jeremy Scott Stankan, you are my dreamboat. I am forever grateful that God brought us together through a series of equally yoked, less than stellar choices that led us to Him and centering our marriage, our life, and our precious babies around Him. Thank you for sharing your passions for Christ and His bride with me. You are my Moses. Our babies (Rourie, Ivan, and Sukey), thank you for helping me to write without restraint, bounce ideas, and carry a pen, recorder, or laptop wherever we would go, and listening to Momma talk about Jesus and the bride without judgment (and keeping me accountable). Kelly Birkhimer, my *bestest* sister in Christ, my OG for life, you make me better through Him and His endless love. Thank you for your constant support, encouragement, and fierce Italian loyalty. Portage

Community Church, it is your endless love for Jesus and people that inspire me every day to try to encourage the bride of Christ to be a little more like He intended through actions and truth. And finally, to my Boogsy (my mum). You may not be here to celebrate what you know I always wanted to complete, but I know the daily celebration with our Father is even sweeter. Thank you, Boogs, for your love, finding the greatest love of your life in Jesus, and inspiring me in my walk with Him every day. I love you to the moon and the back.

Foreword

I am one of those girls who never seems to get a seat at the table. I don't say this in a self-pitying way. I just have a hard time breaking into social circles or getting included. Although I had high hopes that church would be different, it really wasn't.

I thought I knew the secret to getting "in" at church. I would show up every Sunday with a big smile and speak softly and kindly to everyone I encountered. I would basically wear a sign saying, "I love Jesus, so my life is wonderful," which I was sure would bring people in droves asking me to be their friend. People were nice and probably liked me, but I still wasn't getting invited into their lives. Time for a new plan! My next idea was to go with my long-standing routine of being a good girl.

Part of my testimony is that I'm a "reformed good girl." I spent most of my life chasing goodness or at least my idea of goodness. I got really good at it. I worked vigilantly to be good. I avoided conflict at all cost, and I would *never* reveal my messy life—especially at church! I raised my hand to volunteer for anything and everything. I was *super* helpful, *super* available, and *super* happy to be there! People liked that. I got all kinds of compliments like "You are the best Kelly" and "What in the world would we do without you, Kelly?" That felt good, and I wanted more of it. So I kept working. I enjoyed the illusion of being included, but I was exhausted and overextended.

Then I had a big problem. I realized I still wasn't really invited into these people's lives. I was invited to work. I was invited to help them accomplish their mission, but I wasn't really invited to be their friend. If I wasn't of any use, would they just forget my name? After all that work, I wasn't anymore included than I was before. Plain and simple: I just wasn't enough. Enter hurt. Followed by its friend, bitterness.

First of all, I'll answer yes to the obvious question. Do I know that most of this battle was inside my own mind? Well, I do now! But at the time, I was just hurt. I felt let down by my church and every person who attended. I spent my whole life being left out and now, even at a church, people were still hurting me and leaving me out, *right*?

Remember I said that part of my testimony was about being a "reformed good girl." Let me tell you what Jesus did. Jesus sent me Loni. At first, Loni was just another friend I could fool. I put on my "I'm fine" mask. "I'm good, my life is good, my marriage is good … I am a good girl!" But the longer we were friends and the closer we got, it was hard to shield her from seeing my mess. As I was going through this turmoil in my church life and the bitterness grew, it took over other areas of my life. It seeped into my marriage and into my workplace. I couldn't stop myself from sharing this with Loni, and she listened. And guess what happened. I dropped the good girl routine, and she loved me anyway. It was wonderful but shocking.

And then I started learning a few things.

- There is this really powerful word: *no.* I didn't have to say yes to everything I was asked to do. In fact, I wasn't supposed to. All this bitterness I built up because I felt used was my fault. If I was serving because I wanted something out of it for myself, and felt disappointed, that was my fault. And I wasn't being blessed by my acts because I was doing them out of obligation or selfish desires, not for the glory of God.

- Service isn't about me. And it *really* isn't about getting people to like me. When I was so quick to raise my hand, did I ever stop to pray if it was God's will? Or was I too much in a rush to get that attagirl from people. Serving God out of a sense of obligation or duty, apart from love for God, is not what He desires. Serving God should be our natural, love-filled response to Him who loved us first. God the Father instilled in me special gifts and talents, and they are to be used to further His kingdom, not my agenda.

- When I'm faced with "What about me?" thoughts, I should ask, "What about others?" When I was busy feeling so bad for myself for not being invited, I never asked myself, "Who am I inviting to my table?" Who was I seeking out to love and serve, not for my own benefit but because that was what God commanded me to do.
- Loni doesn't play around. She is loving, she is patient, and she is kind. She will build you up and shower you with love, but she will deliver truth that people need to hear. She is a student of God's word and doesn't make light of what God expects her to do with it. She is that 3 a.m. friend who will pick you up in the middle of nowhere if you need her to, but she will also refuse to allow you to drown in your own sin.

I had a recent revelation about one of my stories of bitterness toward my church. I always wanted someone from the church to be my Christian mentor. I wanted to be invited into a close, authentic relationship by an older, wiser woman who would walk with me as I grew closer to Christ. Full disclosure: I never asked for it. I never called the church office and asked for a mentor. I'm not sure I even spoke about it out loud. But I craved it nonetheless. And when I didn't get it, I was hurt, angry, and eventually bitter. Fast-forward to recent months and I had a younger woman ask me to mentor her. I was thrilled to say yes. I told her that this was something I had always wanted but never received, so I would be happy to fill that role for her. As I prayed and prepared to be a mentor, I was thinking about how great this would have been if I had only had a mentor. And I had one of those moments when I felt God stir and these words filled my mind: "You did have it, Kelly. I gave you Loni."

Oh my goodness. All those years I was bitter about never getting my mentor, I had one all along. She may not have been older, but she was wiser. She knew the Bible more than anyone I knew, and she dedicated herself to always doing God's will. She wasn't perfect and never pretended to be. She ran toward brokenness and showed people Jesus. She wasn't obsessed with being liked; she was obsessed with obeying the Father and doing kingdom work.

Loni taught me a lot about Jesus, and I finally got invited. She invited me to be on the board of directors for nonprofit youth outreach. This role had me working with youth, teaching them about Jesus, serving others in His name, and ultimately just loving others. She invited me to be a speaker at a women's conference for over two hundred women. She invited me to pray out loud in front of groups, a big deal for me! She invited me to pray with her and for her. She invited me to see her mess, which made me comfortable enough to share mine. And she loved me through it all. She loved me, she loved my family, and she holds me accountable and corrects me according to God's word. Her greatest act of love: she prays *for* me.

My prayer for anyone reading this book is the same

one I have for my own daughters: may God deliver you a Loni. I promise you it's a game changer. And I almost missed it! I was so busy enjoying her friendship and her all around awesomeness that I missed the fact that she was an undeniable answer to prayer. God delivered exactly what I was asking for; it just wasn't in the way I expected. It came in a way of an authentic, beautiful friendship.

This "reformed good girl" eventually learned a really important lesson. Goodness apart from God is nothing. It's empty, meaningless, and nothing more than busywork that leaves you feeling tired. And I learned that a church isn't a country club. I don't go there and "pay my dues" and then get what I need. That shift in my thinking changed everything. The fact that I don't have to do anything but build a relationship with the One who made me. Through that relationship, God will place desires in my heart to serve in specific places. God's goodness is what I chase after, and I'll go where He sends me. *I* am the church, and I am blessed.

When I first read this book, I joked with Loni that "this book is gonna start a revolution." I have no idea if that's true. But I know one thing: it should. It should revolutionize how we think of the church. It's time for all of us to listen with new ears. Jesus, make new wine out of me.

Kelly Birkhimer

Introduction

When I first began writing this labor of love nearly two years ago, my role and position in ministry was as a lead pastor at a small-town community church. What led to the writing of this book was because this particular body within the body of Christ was different. There was *something* special about that little, tiny church that was getting noticed by their town, community, other churches, and nearby communities. From the moment my family and I stepped into that church on their first Sunday in a building that was freely given to them, I could feel love pouring from the people in those seats. This body was fully seeking God's heart. They were seeking Jesus fully and completely in the Spirit. They were different. Every social class, social misfit, and social butterfly was represented in the few gathered in this beautifully dated church, and what was even more special is that each one felt loved by the other: unified love. Christ truly was and *is* the center of this body of Christ. This outpouring of love and acceptance with *eventual* and *occasional* discipline was unlike anything I had observed or experienced in all the other large and small churches I had attended over the years. This group of believers was seeking Jesus first and loving others as Christ and as the bride. And with each other, they were seeking authentic community and friendship. I watched the leaders and the founders of this church embrace the social elite and the drug addict, the altruistic and the thief, the thriving and the downtrodden every single Sunday.

Their unconditional, never-ending mercy and grace-filled love is what prompted a stirring in my heart (along with some nudging from the Spirit) for the American church. This book isn't a fix-all, fixer-upper, Messiah complex kind of book. This book is just wisdom and advice from living and walking faith out with other believers. This book is to help redefine the hurt church into the divine definition of the bride of Christ as the Father intended.

After reviewing my written, disheveled rambling of my thoughts and heart for over a year, I decided to keep the chapters as they were written during the present time they were conceived. Why? Because it is a true reflection of how we, as the body of Christ, should be ever seeking, ever changing, ever willing to adapt to the love and calling He places on us moment by moment and day by day, yet unwilling to change or adapt our faith as placed with the Father, the Son, and the Holy Spirit.

My heart of heart prayers is for you, whoever is willing, to challenge your perception and role of the traditional

American church and rise up from our megachurches to megacommunities filled with love and grace rooted in the love of Christ and *unified* in one mind and one spirit.

> Therefore, if you have any encouragement from being united with Christ, if any comfort from his love, if any common sharing in the Spirit, if any tenderness and compassion, then make my joy complete by being like-minded, having the SAME love, being ONE in spirit and of ONE mind.[1]

After all, an old Swahili proverb says, "Where there is unity, there is strength. But where there is division, there is weakness." Church, isn't it time to become an army of one rooted in love, joy, peace, patience, goodness, gentleness, faithfulness, and self-control?[2]

---

[1] Philippians 2:1–2; capitalization for emphasis on "ONE."
[2] Galatians 5:22–23; I seriously made my son memorize this when he was two and a tyrant.

Chapter

ONE

"Pastor" carries heavy weight to the one who bears it and for the one who hears it. There are so many negative and positive connotations with that title. Recently, I experienced bearing the weight of this title when someone flippantly (and in a huff) blurted, *"You are the pastor?"*

And to their unbelief, the answer was yes. Honestly, the answer I state is often in disbelief to me as well. My journey with Christ did not start at a young age, in a Christian home, with a Christian family, with the typical American-Christian dream, or with Christianese being prayed over me. Nope. I was born into a broken home, a broken mess, and had no real understanding of relationships, especially the life-giving kind. Life did not start this way for me. I wasn't born a pastor. I wasn't born complete. My journey with Christ began exactly where it needed to—at the altar. Notably, the altar is a place of sacrifice. And at that altar of sacrifice, I had to make a decision. I was either going to continue to do it my way, which quite frankly was not working for me, or I was going to try it God's way. And truth be told, I was completely oblivious to my beautiful mess well into my early adulthood, until I finally came to the realization that I was in fact broken, missing pieces, and seeking something more.

The abandonment I experienced as a child led to a series of adolescent, teen, and young adult choices that were less than worthy and lots of censoring.[3] However, it's this worthlessness that led me right to the arms of the Savior. When all the other arms around me were extended, reaching, and seeking, it was the arms of the Savior who gave me exactly what I needed: remembered, forgiven, and loved. It was not into the arms of the church. It was into the arms of the Savior where I found wholeness and completeness. I ran to the church on countless occasions, and although so many of those churchgoers meant well, I left most Sundays, when I attended, emptier than before. Why? Because I was also defeated, deflated, and convinced, not about God's gracious, unending, reckless love. I was going to have to work a lot harder to see the Savior of the world instead of a fiery pit.

---

[3] This is worth a footnote because seriously, I could write a book on "what *not* to do" or "how to perfect 'bad.'"

I was scared. I was scared to disappoint the ones around me. I didn't want to disappoint my pastors. I didn't want to disappoint my Sunday school teachers with the fact that, yet again, I was running into the arms of the world instead of the Savior. I didn't want to disappoint God. So I worked and worked and worked to make sure the people around me would see the "good" things I did. And this would make the God of the universe see me, be pleased, and keep me from the fiery pit too. Again, none of these people meant to lead me on this path of pleasing man, but they, too, were trying to please man. This is what the church had become—dress up, show up, pay up, perform up, then maybe you could go up. They were in love with the pastor, the building, the musical performance, the *spiritual* show, and the number of filled seats because that shows success. And this is where we are as the American church.

Too many "Christians" and those speaking with eloquent language are nothing more than banging gongs and empty cymbals. "I am only a resounding gong or clanging cymbal."[4] We have forgotten the most important part in our walk, in our unworthiness, and the calling God has placed on our lives—each of us: the calling to love unconditionally those who are just as unworthy as our humble beginnings. And as a church, we are failing to love like Jesus in so many ways. From our teachings

---

[4] 1 Corinthians 13:1 (NIV). Read this chapter again and again. This is so much more than a love chapter overly recited at weddings.

to preachings, to children ministries and financial and building status, we have forgotten the basic elements of church.

> They devoted themselves to the apostles' teachings and to the fellowship, to the breaking of bread and to prayer. Everyone was filled with awe at the many wonders and signs performed by the apostles. All the believers were together and had everything in common. They sold property and possessions to give to anyone who had need. Every day they continued to meet together in the temple courts. They broke bread in their homes and ate together with glad and sincere hearts, praising God and enjoying the favor of all the people. And the Lord added to their number daily those who were being saved.[5]

This was a glimpse of the early church. The basic elements of loving, sharing, standing in awe of the Savior, and meeting people at their needs *with sincere hearts in their homes* has become something foreign within our churches. The result is a hurt church and hurt people. We have lost our kingdom's purpose and most important

---

[5] Acts 2:42–47 (NIV). Basic elements: believe, receive, love, share, worship, and kingdom purpose.

investment: *people*. Our investment has become more about the church building than the people inside. I can remember my grandmother teaching me a nursery rhyme. "Here is the church (hands boxed), here are the steeples (pointer and pinky fingers up), open up the doors (thumbs open), and see all the people (all the other fingers flailing around)."

Today's version would maybe include major sound, lighting, and a coffee bar with multiple business transactions and various financial investments. These "investments" within our churches are not necessarily bad things, but when the investment on these items outweighs meeting the needs of people, simply loving people, our priorities have become skewed and the preaching becomes nothing more than empty words, resounding gongs, and clanging cymbals. "We love because He first loved us."[6] He has called each of us to love. "Love is a battlefield" is more than a great eighties song. (There is such great truth to the benefits of wild hair and makeup.) Loving people as ourselves and loving our neighbors can be a struggle. The reality is this is the first and greatest commandment, and ironically the first one, we neglect.

The church has open doors on Sunday morning, but oftentimes our church doors have a conditional opening. How do you worship? Are you born again? Do you speak in tongues? Do you have a children's ministry lined up with events for my children all summer? Do the children

---

[6] 1 John 4:4 (NIV).

worship with the adults? When do you do communion? Is that person allowed to come here *like that?* Do they even tithe? What is their sexuality? Nationality? Personality? And every other "ality"? And these are just a few of the questions before we get to question one. What do *you*— new, trendy, tattooed, short-haired, single mom, young, old, former prisoner, drunk and out all night, different-from-me—*need?* Imagine if every church first prayed and then asked God to help them to see the *need* of every person who walked through those open doors rather than "How can you serve us?"

I'll never forget one of my first Sundays pastoring in our little church. As I stood front and center preaching about whatever God had laid on my heart that Sunday, I honestly have no idea because of what happened next. A strange man, only because I had never met him, walked through our front doors. No one else in the congregation had noticed except me. So as I continued, I watched him watch me. My "stranger danger" radar began to send signals to my brain as he just continued to stare rather intensely yet indifferently. As I remember that stare, I now know my radar went off because it was the same stare I witnessed my mom endure time and time again from a man who was deciding whether to peacefully slip into his drunken, stupor coma or angrily slip into a fit of abusive rage. My next thought was concerning all the precious kiddos, including my own, in the parsonage right next to us, followed by "What do I do?"

So what did I do? I kept on speaking right through the Spirit and praying silently with the Spirit while attempting not to alarm anyone. Why? Because this man had a need. So I did what I always do in my very socially awkward self. I smiled hugely, drawing attention to this newest member of our congregation. That grabbed the attention of another member, who promptly escorted him to a seat right next to her. This man proceeded to move three more times throughout the service, and I just kept on preaching God's love. At the end of the service, what did our little church do? We insisted he sit with us and have lunch.

He avoided me like the plague, but he bantered with our worship leader and other members without saying his name or wanting to reveal it. He made some remarks about the church being a place that hurt him. And we just kept on physically feeding him and trying to spiritually nourish his soul through unconditional love. I kept on praying and smiling, knowing he was lost, he was hurt, and he was drowning in his own drunkenness. The man left that day more confused and bewildered than when he stumbled into our building inebriated and lost. Why? Because we were not a church building that day; we were the church, the bride, and the love, which met that man's need at that appointed time. When he left, my prayer was that at least he had just a glimpse of Jesus that day.

Months later, I found out just what we did that day. The man was on a broken and worn-out path of destruction. And although he is still struggling, his only comment about that day, with several apologies, was our little church was different. He didn't feel judged and wasn't thrown out, and if he was coming back to church, he knew where to go. I haven't seen him return yet, but I know there's a place at the table when he decides to join us.[7]

What did we do? We loved him first. Did I do that on my own? Oh, heck no. I couldn't in my power because I was staring at a man who looked like my past, smelled like my past, and my brain was figuring out how to escape if I needed to protect my babies, friends, and members of our church family. Instead of judging, I prayed. Instead of pointing out his sin, I prayed. Instead of worrying, I prayed. And what did I pray? I prayed to meet this man at his most simple *need*. He needed someone to listen, to feel accepted, and to eat a hot meal before he had to face his sobering reality again. And that is exactly what we did.

What did Jesus do for Paul? Peter? Matthew? Mary? He met each one of them at his or her need. He didn't question what or why or judge each sin first. He simply met them at each of their needs. You want fish? Done. You want a friend? Done. You want forgiveness? Done. You need healed? Done. There weren't any conditions set on his love or the amount of love he gave to them or to each of us. He

---

[7] Read "The Last Supper" in Matthew 26:17–30 or in Mark 14:12–31 (NIV). Jesus ate with *all* twelve disciples, the imperfect men. One would betray Him and help lead to His death and the other who was faithful and loyal would deny him three times, yet all were invited to the table: the sinners and the saints.

just loved. Why? Because how else do you get people to the Father? How else do you explain the love the Creator of the universe has, especially after the Old Testament? (I love the Old Testament—just saying there was a lot of death and destruction.)[8]

Everyone's beginning looks different. Some of us love Jesus from the moment we can say His name, some of us never recognize or accept that free act of love, and there are some (like me) who take the tortoise trail. Either way, our end is the same if we are reading this and have given our life and our love to the one who paid it all.

Jesus looked different. He didn't come from the same societal upbringings and cloth that the Pharisees had been birthed in, and he certainly didn't wear their portentous garb. Jesus had humble beginnings in that manger, on the side of the mountain, without the same amenities that had been afforded to the church leaders of the day. He was different.

Many of our churches today have forgotten their humble beginnings. Church started somewhere for many of our American church leaders, whether that was in a basement, in an established building, or with a specific religious entity; the calling to serve in ministry began somewhere. It may have even been in a person's darkest moment,[9] an hour that the Holy Spirit called and led that person to the light

---

[8] For an obvious place and purpose—no judgment on the judges.

[9] Check out Heman the Ezrahite in Psalm 88. Wow! Darkest moments but highest praise.

directly to God's perfect glory, or it could have been the calling from generation to generation. Either way, church leaders all over America have a story about what led them to serve the church.

Paul has a story. John has a story. James has a story. Peter has a story. Since the beginning of the first church when Christians were titled "Christians" in Antioch, each of us has a story. But as our numbers grow, buildings grow, the bank account grows, problems begin to grow too, and investments and consumers change. And this nasty little thing called "pride" grows right along with it. We forget the humble beginnings of the church, our church, the people in the church, and their stories of loss and redemption. We forget that church is not a building; it is the people. We forget what it means to love like Jesus, serve like Jesus, and to be the hands and feet of Jesus.

This is not an expert manual on how to "church." I am certainly not the number one church leader in America; honestly, sometimes I don't know if I even like "church."[10] But what I do know is that I love God, and I love people. I know that I love to meet people right where they are and to "do church" wherever that might be. I know I have a desire and drive to see people fall in love with Jesus, to step into his or her kingdom purpose, and to one day praise our

---

[10] Before you stop reading and make horrible assumptions about my faith, please note that I love the Acts church and God's intentions for what He wanted the bride of Christ to be. Keep reading. You'll get me later—I hope.

Father in heaven with people from all over the world in different areas, in different languages, in song and dance—one melodious tune and dance honoring the Creator of the universe. I hope that is your desire too. And where does it start? With us. With us redefining what the church has become. With us coming back to the basics. With us remembering who we are as the church—the bride of Christ.

My journey with Christ began exactly where it needed to: at the altar. And at that altar of sacrifice, I had to make a decision. We have to make the decision as a church as well: do we do it our way or God's way?

Chapter
TWO

How many times have you invited someone to church, a special service, a conference, or something that is church or church related? How many times have you invited someone to coffee, lunch, dinner, or just a simple walk? Out of the times you have invited someone to church or to just meet them somewhere to catch up or chat, how often did they respond yes to church?

Church membership is below 50 percent[11] and those who attend church is at an all-time low of 23 percent regular weekly attendees.[12] Most millennials claim to have "never"

---

[11] Jones, Jeffrey. Gallup. "US Church Membership Falls below Majority for First Time." 2021. https://news.gallup.com.

[12] Statista Research Department. Church Attendance of Americans 2021. 2021. https://www.statista.com.

even attended church or a religious service. However, and interestingly, Christianity is exploding in Africa, South America, and Asia, where it is doubling the rate of growth in Europe and America.[13] But why? Most of these Southern Hemisphere countries have been heavily hit with missionaries for decades. The missionaries are not *inviting* the natives to church; they are *going* to them. They are meeting the needs of the people in the poorest areas around the world, loving them, and sharing the gospel and truth of Jesus while meeting their simplest yet direst needs.

> One day as Jesus was standing by the Lake of Gennesaret, the people were crowding around him and listening to the word of God. He saw at the water's edge two boats, left there by the fishermen, who were washing their nets. He got into one of the boats, the one belonging to Simon, and asked him to put out a little from shore. Then he sat down and taught the people from the boat. When he had finished speaking, he said to Simon, "Put out into deep water, and let down the nets for a catch."
>
> Simon answered, "Master, we've worked hard all night and haven't caught anything.

---

[13] Lifeway Research. 7 Surprising Trends in Global Christianity. 2019. https://lifewayresearch.com.

But because you say so, I will let down the nets." When they had done so, they caught such a large number of fish that their nets began to break. So they signaled their partners in the other boat to come and help them, and they came and filled both boats so full that they began to sink. When Simon Peter saw this, he fell at Jesus' knees and said, "Go away from me, Lord; I am a sinful man!" For he and all his companions were astonished at the catch of fish they had taken, and so were James and John, the sons of Zebedee, Simon's partners. Then Jesus said to Simon, "Don't be afraid; from now on you will fish for people." So they pulled their boats up on shore, left everything and followed him.[14]

Wow! What a beautiful picture of meeting people at their needs. This is what Jesus did, and this is what we are called to do. There are many reasons why our American churches are failing, and some of that failure has to do with meeting the needs of the budget rather than the needs directly outside the four walls of the church building. Don't misjudge here, but I have heard several churchgoers and board members more worried about the salary of

---

[14] Luke 5:1–11 (NIV).

the charismatic pastor than the missionary budget, and more churchgoers and onlookers concerned about the state-of-the-art sound system than providing tools to the congregation to meet needs and others with the message of the love of Christ. We are performing up rather than preparing up.

I recently read that the "megachurch" sites in Africa are morphing into cities. The megachurch isn't a building. It has become a kingdom with its own banks, hospitals, schools, and police systems all working toward building the church body not the physical church building. And what is even more spectacular is that this movement, this conversion, started in the hearts of missionaries wanting to bring people to the kingdom, wanting to see kingdom purpose and growth, and now infiltrating entire countries in Africa to full conversion to the Christian faith—to the love of Christ and the sovereignty of God. They met people on their turf, on their field, in their house, on their lawn, for coffee, on a walk, with groceries, a hand to hold, or arms to hold too many babies, and shoulders to help carry the weight. Jesus was rejected by the church but built the kingdom. Jesus called His first disciples not by an invite to the church that rejected Him but by meeting simple fishermen at their greatest need—with fish.

Cast your nets,
just check to see.
Maybe you missed a spot in the sea—
Done.

Jesus caught those fishermen hook, line, and sinker, right there at their greatest need. They didn't even have to move to find Him.

Chapter
THREE

S o as I sit here and work on this glimpse of what I want and see for the future of Christ's bride, "the church," I want to share what my husband is doing. But before I do that, I think you should know a couple things about Jeremy Scott Stankan. He is kind but also opinionated. He loves to talk and expects immediate rebuttal. He is a fixer but also makes a whole lot of mess. He is fiercely loyal to his family and faith. He is my biggest supporter on this side of heaven, and most importantly (and why this whole book thing started), he loves Jesus but not the current state of the church.

So what is he currently doing? He is currently dragging (literally dragging in a giant blue holding tank) human waste to the sewage dump. Why? Because we (his wife and three children) have used the camper facilities without being directly connected to a sewage dump and between said wife, three children, and numerous friends, all have managed to fill the camper facility. How does this very blemished mess have anything to do with the unblemished bride of Christ? Well, my husband is dumping the tank because before this process occurred, he made the unselfish commitment to dump whatever made it into that reservoir because he just unconditionally loves us and wanted to make our lives and those of the ones we love and our friends a little easier when using the potty at camp. This may not seem like a big deal, but listen: poop is always a big deal (especially when it is not your own). And the cap on the holding tank broke, so you can imagine the amount of sloshing and mess this whole unselfish act of kindness and generosity has created. Not to mention the blown tire on the 4.5-hour drive to camp, the twisted bumper jack, and the messed-up sway bars before we left.

Church is messy, gross, and full of a whole lot of human waste. Or at least it should be. I would much rather attend church with real, authentic, messy humans than play dress-up on Sunday. For the longest time, my answer to anyone who asked how I was, how things were going, or how my family was was always "Living the dream." And although I do think that most of my life with Jesus (although imperfect but perfect with Him) is awesome, it is not always dreamy. Many of our American churches have become places to live this imaginary dream. We put on the suits or skinny jeans, smiles, and handshakes and walk into church imagining or pretending this perfect life. We enjoy great entertainment and a speaker and go home empty. Imagine if we got real. Imagine if we looked people in the eye and expected and received truth. Imagine if you could actually tell your pastor how you really feel or ask the greeter to pray with you because you just spent the last five minutes in your car as mad as a hornet.[15] Imagine if we could be the one place in the world of selfies and farce that people could be honest.

Jesus was messy. Jesus had gross feet (seriously a carpenter with sandals walking) a lot. Jesus carried a whole lot of human waste (in fact *all of humanity's* on the cross), and he never wore skinny jeans or a suit. His life wasn't dreamy. His life was real. He didn't provide great entertainment. He provided unconditional love, truth, and miracles. And the best part: He encouraged those around Him to do the same thing: to get real. He didn't tell Matthew to get it together before he decided to follow Him around. He didn't tell the fisherman to stop living sinfully before they attended a Jesus meeting. And He certainly didn't expect any of them to hide the truth; in fact, they couldn't. Jesus knew right where they were and where they were going, and He loved them anyway. He knew Peter would deny Him even after knowing Him, even after spending quality time with the Savior of the world, yet Jesus loved

---

[15] About your morning, your spouse, your children, the driver who clearly obeys the traffic laws to the fault of making you late to church.

Peter and met Peter exactly where Peter was every time. Our church culture has become very good with placing church responsibilities, duties, and taking care of the poor and widows on a few people in the church so that the rest of us can just show up, dress up, pay up, and perform up, and we have done our duty for the church. This just isn't what God intended. When Jesus discusses serving the widows, children, and loving our enemy, that is for all of us—not the few we label as "church leaders." Loving isn't easy. Loving unconditionally is tough and messy. People are messy. But if we want to see the church become the bride of Christ, it is time to get real.

Every Tuesday we have prayer and Bible study at church. This group has grown to at times having more people than we have on a single Sunday church service. Why? Because all are welcome to attend—from no church, to any church, young and old (or more marinated), believers and unbelievers or someone who is seeking. It doesn't matter. We encourage all to attend wherever we can. This group has prayed for our smaller community to the nation and global, for the church—local, national, global, for the free and the addict, for our friends, family, and complete strangers. I have had the opportunity to meet people in our little parsonage that I will never meet within our four walls of church (yet). Why? Because people are nervous about church; we have failed them. Left them bitter. Expected too much. Everyone is a little too "OK" and "livin' the dream" on a Sunday morning, but in our little parsonage, people become less guarded, less nervous, and get real and honest answers. People know they can come there with their holding tanks full and dirty and leave a little emptier and cleaner. How? Because we hug, laugh, cry, and pray without any knowledge of where they've been, how they got there, their social status or bank accounts, or anything else that doesn't have something to do with meeting them right now. I've seen people come faithfully every Tuesday and those who have never returned, but I know they left a little cleaner and a little less full of the mess and fuller with love and acceptance. And it's not me—the faithful pastor who has that role; it is all of us. It is each of us doing our part as the body to bring others to the fullness and love of the Savior. There are Tuesdays I can't attend between my family and teaching, but the people still come. So no, it is not my dynamic personality. It is the love and commitment to Christ, His kingdom, and so desperately wanting others to know that love that brings friends and strangers every Tuesday.

I left one of our prayer and Bible studies last Tuesday with a former student and started chuckling on the way home. My exact words to her were "Only Jesus could bring together such a misfit group of people to love, pray, and study. Where else do you see such an eclectic group of people all together with the same love and passion?" We giggled, but it resonated deep in my soul. Why? Because that is the church. That is kingdom purpose. That is living a life that doesn't expect to clean out the holding tank but does it anyway.

> Love must be sincere. Hate what is evil; cling to what is good. Be devoted to one another in love. Honor one another above yourselves. Never be lacking in zeal, but keep your spiritual fervor, serving the Lord. Be joyful in hope, patient in affliction, faithful in prayer. Share with the Lord's people who are in need. Practice hospitality.
>
> Bless those who persecute you; bless and do not curse. Rejoice with those who rejoice; mourn with those who mourn. Live in harmony with one another. Do not be proud, but be willing to associate with people of low position. Do not be conceited ...
>
> If your enemy is hungry, feed him; if he is thirsty, give him something to drink ...[16]

Jeremy didn't marry me expecting with excitement to never have to clean up the poop. (Gross, I know.) But the reality is that in our miniscule, messy, beautiful, chaotic fifteen years of marriage, things have been tough and

---

[16] Romans 12:9–20 (NIV). This is love in action. This is cleaning the tank. This should be the bride—always.

dirty. However, with Christ as our center, we clean up the holding tanks. Neither one of us fully entered marriage understanding the other's dirt, mess, and filth. We had to have some difficult talks. We have experienced grief together, anger together, hurt together, and loss together. We've lost a baby, a ministry, and a business. It has been messy, heartbreaking, gut-wrenching, and chaotic. Our marriage has also been honest, kind, selfless, fruitful, and Jesus loving. We have taught and learned to be real, raw, and honest even when we didn't know how the other would respond. This wasn't just one person's role; this was a three-corded braid between Jeremy, me, and the Father.[17]

If we want the same for our church, for the people who attend or who will never step inside those four walls, church, it is time to clean the tank. Let's get dirty.

---

[17] Ecclesiastes 4:12 (NIV). When you need strengthened in a relationship, pull out the braiding skills. Our third strand is always the toughest.

Chapter

FOUR

Jesus loves me this I know, for the Bible tells me so. Little ones to him belong. They are weak, but He is strong. Yes, Jesus loves me. Yes, Jesus loves me. Yes, Jesus loves me. The Bible tells me so.

Jesus loves me this I know, as he loved so long ago. Taking children on his knee, saying, "Let them come to Me." Yes, Jesus loves me. Yes, Jesus loves me. Yes, Jesus loves me. The Bible tells me so.

Jesus loves me still today, walking with me on my way. Wanting as a friend to give light and love to all who live. Yes, Jesus loves me.

Yes, Jesus loves me. Yes, Jesus loves me. The
Bible tells me so.

I think most Christians are very familiar with the
"Jesus Loves Me" song. I know that my husband and I have
sung this to our kiddos from the time they were young.
Although it wasn't until our youngest was born that we
were introduced to the entire song. Since then, I have been
reading and trying to memorize these short verses every
night before bed as I sing her to sleep. During one evening,
as I was reading her these verses for the umpteenth time
and looking at the cute little bear images that accompany
each page, something occurred to me that never had
before. Not on one page of this children's book is there a
picture or painting or illustration of Jesus. Instead, there
are images of a little bear family doing everyday things.
A momma bear and papa bear reading the Bible for the
first time with their little one, fishing for the first time,
checking on the chickens, painting Easter eggs with a small
sign in the kitchen that reads, "Bear with each other and
forgive [in bold letters]," baby bear playing and sharing
with the neighbors, singing, dancing, baking and sharing
(again) the cookies with the friends, and then camping,
walking, and finally carrying each other home to snuggle
in bed finishing the chorus "Yes, Jesus loves me!" And for
the first time, I realized what this little children's book is
illustrating: *us* (you and me albeit through a bear family)
sharing the love of Jesus with all of those around us. Not

Jesus walking and singing these verses to little ones, but *us*. You and I empowered by the Spirit and enamored by the love of Christ fellowshipping and sharing, "Yes, Jesus loves me! Yes, Jesus loves you! Yes, Jesus loves us! The Bible tells me so." And this is the illustration of Jesus. I guess He was in there after all.

I know this may seem like a lot from a children's book, but doesn't this speak volumes about how difficult we make scripture? We have managed to misrepresent, misspeak, misinterpret, and just plain miss the mark on the word of God. Pastors and leaders have become superfluous and winded concerning God's word in direct relation to opinion, politics, the purse, and agenda. We preach Jesus but fail to show Him, fail to walk like Him, fail to love like Him, and fail to be His bride.

Simply stated, God is good. God is love. God is sovereign. His ways are not our ways. His ways are better. His love is better. By the way, God loves you. *Period.* Obviously, there is a lot more to the intricately and beautifully written words of the greatest love story on earth, but we have managed to overcomplicate and cast judgment based on our opinions of His word than His actual words. There are lessons in the parables and lessons in the Old Testament. Just read any one of the prophets. But what we have managed to do is single-handedly fight one another on every last detail of every last word of a Bible that has been written and interpreted hundreds if not thousands of times from its original text. We have got caught up in everything from the gifts of the

Spirit (who has them and who doesn't) to blowing a ram horn in church for the spiritually elite, from spiritually dry to spiritually silly, from helping the needy to bashing the welfare system, from a hospital of sinners to the cathedral of saints, and from praying for our leaders to a political circus. And yes, we have managed to misuse and misrepresent God's word to prove the agenda or opinion we support for each one. As a result, we now have the slowest-growing and quickest-dying Christian population in the world. And through the midst of our chaos and judgment, we still want people to know that Jesus loves them—*if* you are a certain religion. *If* you have the gifts of the spirit (especially the one He says is the least of these).[18] *If* you vote for a certain political party because obviously one is closer and privier to God's selection than the other. *If* you go to church on Sunday and make sure you pay your 10 percent—an every-weeker and not a Chreaster. *If* you are good and do good things. Don't forget to do, do, do. *If. If. If.* You get the idea.

When looking up information concerning the fastest-growing Christian population on the planet, it was not shocking to me that it was those nations needing, expecting, and clinging to the one thing missionaries were bringing them: the love of Christ. They were met with Jesus every time someone showed up to feed them, clothe them, provide medicine, hold babies, and just plain love them. It was the

---

[18] Check out 1 Corinthians 12–14. There is so much to learn about the gifts, but spoiler alert: the greatest gift is love.

love (much like the bear family) that brought them straight to the loving arms of Jesus. They were loved right there in the mess, dirt, filth, and chaos. They didn't need the multiple variants of what one scripture meant to another. They didn't need the theology of the elders. They just needed one thing: God loves you. God sent His Son. Jesus loves you. I love you. *Period.*

The rest comes naturally when you fully know, love, and grasp the vastness of the Savior. The Holy Spirit leads the way when we are filled with God's truth, not man's agenda.

Don't misunderstand me. I study the Bible. I study truth. I look at multiple texts, versions, interpretations, and then I pray—my most significant tool. As a church, we recently studied the book of Job on Sunday mornings and Tuesday Bible studies. What struck me about Job and the advice he received from his friends was the bad theology—the elementary thinking about God and who He is. We have become much like Job's friends Eliphaz, Bildad, and Zophar believing in elementary theology that if we love God and do good things, we can expect good rewards. And when we don't love God or do good things, then we can expect bad consequences and bad rewards. This elementary thinking is just not true. Job was a man (much like my dreamy husband, I hope) who was found blameless in the sight of God. In fact, it was this blamelessness that prompted God to ask Satan if he had ever considered his man, Job. If you're not familiar with Job, read it, but for those of you who know, you know what happens next. This prompts Job, quite possibly the richest leader of the time, to lose his wealth, family, and health almost instantaneously. Job's faith is rocked. It is shaken. And his "friends" have no problem trying to force Job into repentance because good people get good rewards and bad people get suffering and shame, so clearly Job did something wrong. For several chapters, they fail to listen to Job and push their bad theology instead.

Isn't this what we too have done? We have pushed people into thinking that they better have it all together. This isn't something we as a church have intentionally done. This is something that has simmered and marinated for many years: if you love Jesus, then you are always happy, always smiling, your marriage is better, your job is better, your kiddos are better, etc. You are just better *or you'd better be smiling when you meet with others, attend church, do the events, and just appear happy.* Why? Because somewhere along the way of faulty theology, we have mistaken Christ's joy with the world's happiness. They'd better be smiling (at least on the outside) when they come to church. To love Jesus means we are put together inside and out. Our hands don't have to get dirty being the church. Just step inside our new state-of-the-art facility. We have managed to sweep major problems under the proverbial carpet to make sure we keep the stereotypical look of the American church. I know many people who have left the Catholic faith because of the years of abuse that was swept away and neglected by the leaders of the church. I also know many of those people not only left the church but left Jesus. Churched people are hurt people.

"I can do all things through Christ who gives me strength" is one of the most misquoted, overused, and misused scripture I have heard throughout the years. Most people fail to read the verses before Philippians 3:14. In verses 12 and 13, Paul lets us know that we can be content in little and in much. Our contentment (true joy in the good and the bad, with little and with much) is only rooted in Jesus. Having a bad day doesn't mean we smile on the outside and weep inside. What if instead of faking till we make it we stopped, prayed, and sought our church family to pray with us, to stand in the gap for us, and to love us in the good and the bad, in sickness and in health, regardless of our situation or circumstances?

What if our *ifs* changed? What if our *ifs* became solid words built on a foundation of truth? What if instead of *ifs*, we simply said, "Jesus loves me, this I know, for the Bible tells me so. Jesus loves you, this I know, for the Bible tells me so." Period.

Chapter
FIVE

The thief comes only to steal and kill and destroy; I have come that they may have life, and have it to the full.

—John 10:10

A gain, I can't take any credit for this chapter. During a service one Sunday morning, I told the congregation that my husband was my Moses and I was his Aaron. I am fairly certain I may have spoken that into existence. Seriously.

During summer as my husband was catching up on some work in his shop below the house, John 10:10 began taking root in his heart. We had a rough 2020 as most people experienced and his business felt the effects of the pandemic in many different ways. During the summer of 2021 when those effects began to show, and even as I write this, we have had to face some pretty difficult choices. In the midst of those choices, there were others involved in this process who have also played an influential part in shutting down the business. Obviously, being the upright and upstanding Christians we are, we have name-called,[19] pointed fingers, been frustrated, and just been plain angry (not me—just Jeremy[20]). So in all of our *very* righteous filled aggression, the Holy Spirit hit Jeremy with John 10:10. Only this time, this well-known scripture hit a bull's-eye in his heart. The enemy comes to do these things. It is scriptural. We know it to be true, but how does he do this? He accomplishes these things through God's people! We often steal, kill, and destroy others without thinking about this scripture for a second because *we don't do that.* The enemy does! We may not physically steal someone's belongings, commit murder, or destroy someone's physical property, but when was the last time we name-called? Got angry with another slow driver or told someone how ridiculous their decision was or that they did something wrong—again? Gossiped about someone and destroyed a person's self-esteem or lost the trust of a friend because we just *had* to tell someone else about that person's problem so we could "pray" for them? How often have you been angry at a business call, a coach's call, or a call from your spouse or friend?

---

[19] Clearly sarcastic here. Don't name-call. It just isn't nice.

[20] OK, also not true, but pastors never do any of those heathen things, right?

We steal, kill, and destroy each other more often than I would care to admit. And it wasn't until my Moses (Jeremy) pointed this scripture to me that I even gave this a thought. We are always justifying and protecting our thoughts, intentions, and actions because life isn't fair, and *aren't we allowed to have an opinion based on the circumstances around us?*

But what if, before the berede of words, thoughts, and actions, we stopped and remembered this scripture? What if we rose above the circumstances to fresh perspective like Habakkuk who climbs the wall of Jerusalem[21] to really see the people, the events, the situation before speaking and acting? What if we realized when we are being the enemy?

Job's three friends needed a fresh perspective about Job. Instead of assuming, berating, and condemning, they needed to pray. Words were not needed; they just needed to pray right there in the town dump with their bestie. Eliphaz, Bildad, and Zophar were stealing, killing, and destroying their friend's hope, encouragement, integrity, character, and faith—all in the name of God and their assumptions about why God does what He does. Rather than lifting a man who had lost his children, servants, wealth, and health and was literally sitting in his own ashes in the town dump being mocked and lambasted by those who once stopped and listened to this man of God, they assumed Job had sinned

---

[21] Habakkuk is a minor prophet in the Old Testament. Give him a serious read! We all have walls to climb!

and then placed their elementary theology on a blameless (not sinless) chosen man of God. They pointed fingers, made false assumptions, name-called, and were just mean. They didn't listen to Job's rebuttal. They didn't remember that Job was upright and moral—blameless in the sight of God. Nope. They just assumed and became exactly what the devil intended: the enemy. "The enemy comes to steal, kill and destroy" (John 10:10). How often have we, as followers of Christ, done the same thing?

"I have come that they may have life, and have it to the full."[22] Have you? Have you approached a friend in need with this attitude? Have you approached a friend with advice based on their situation and what you assume, or have you approached a friend, above their circumstances, with the love of Christ, full of life, and wanting them to live that full life too?

Several years ago, I approached a dear friend with this same elementary theology. This was a friend who was near and dear to my heart, and she came to visit. I had a rich past with this friend and her family. I always desired for this family to come to the Lord and for this friend to *change her ways.* As we were chatting, I proceeded to tell her how much better my life was (than hers), how much peace I had (above hers), and how much I do (above most) in all my self-righteousness. I thought if I could just make this sinner see her ways, then she would want to stop sinning

---

[22] John 10:10 (NIV).

(just like me—*clearly),* go to church, and love Jesus. In the middle of my tirade, she stopped me and said, "Loni, I live a good life and do nice things for people because I love them. I don't need you to tell me why I need to be 'good' and do 'good' things. I already do because that is who I am." Needless to say, our visit ended rather abruptly, and she walked away from our friendship. Years later, the Lord brought this moment back to my memory. Why? Because I had it (my faith) and I had Him all wrong. "As Jesus was walking by the Sea of Galilee, he saw two brothers, Simon called Peter and his brother Andrew. They were casting a net into the lake, for they were fishermen. 'Come, follow me,' Jesus said, 'and I will send you out to fish for people.' At once, they left their nets and followed him."[23]

I wasn't following Christ. I was following a set of laws, rules, and instructions rather than allowing the God of the universe, and His Holy Spirit, to guide me, lead me, and instruct me. I was looking at the Bible as an instruction manual built on rules, laws, and ifs instead of love, grace, and absolutes. I missed the mark when it came to following Him, setting the net, and allowing Him to do the rest. My intentions were good. I wanted my friend to know Jesus. But my approach was bad: follow what I do to self-righteousness. I was stuck in a kindergarten theology of good people are rewarded and sinful people suffer. Instead of loving my friend right where she was, *showing* her how my life had

---

[23] Matthew 4:18–20 (NIV).

been changed, I was pushing rules and theology on deaf ears. I was telling her all the things and sins she shouldn't be doing to save her from the pit instead of why my life had been completely changed because of the love of the Savior. I missed telling her how the Living God, the Creator of the universe, had enough time to see me, meet me, and save me. Instead of relationship building, I was in relationship demo.

Isn't that where many of us are in our faith or stuck in our faith: bad kindergarten theology? We aren't loving; we are condemning. If that person is suffering, it is because of their lack of faith or sin. I was stuck in the rules instead of in the relationship. I wasn't fishing for people; I was fishing for my own self-righteousness with my holy net. When I think of this friend, I pray for her. I pray for her family. I pray someone with the love of Christ and love for people will enter her life and deliver the message of the good news without the conviction and condemnation that I delivered so many years ago. I pray that person will be full of the Spirit and love her right where she is as a beautiful daughter of Christ, so that her heart will be open to receive all God has for her and His good and perfect plan for her life.

The enemy used me that day to steal, kill, and destroy my friend's worth and kindness and cleverly disguised it as an attempt to bring her to God in all my self—righteousness and *sinless*[24] life. Since then, my God has gently reminded me

---

[24] Umm, I am still a sinner. I am working on it though—till the day of completion.

of who I am in Him in various times using that particular situation. I will do everything I can in the power of Spirit to make sure that doesn't happen again. There is a song by Anne Wilson titled "My Jesus" that has the line "Let my Jesus change your life." I needed that song in my heart all those years ago. It is not our job as followers of Christ, as a church body, to change someone's life, perspective, attitude, or anything else we don't agree with. It *is* our job to love God and then love others like Jesus. Matthew 4:19 tells us to follow Jesus and then He will make us fishers of men. Imagine if as a church body we did just that: followed him, cast the bait of our life, and reeled people into the kingdom because of the love, grace, and mercy bait that Jesus supplied from His tackle box instead of our own bait filled with judgment and condemnation.

In many conversations over the past few years, most people have left the church not because of *lack of who Jesus is* but because of the *lack of who He is within the "churched" people*. Rather than allowing the enemy to use us to steal, kill, and destroy, let's choose to let Jesus give us life and use it fully!

Chapter SIX

When the Advocate comes, whom I will
send to you from the Father—the Spirit
of truth who goes out from the Father—
he will testify about me. And you must
testify, for you have been with me from the
beginning.

—John 15:26 (NIV)

I have had the opportunity to be a part of a charismatic
church where a Sunday morning service looked a lot
like Sunday evening football and someone was getting
slain somewhere on that playing field. I have also had the
opportunity to be a part of a church where lifting your
hands in praise got a few wondrous stares. Between the
two, there is a lot of confusion and stress about how to

behave in church, and quite frankly, it is because we have forgotten our who. We have either become spiritually hyped or spiritually dry and right in the middle is Jesus. We have forgotten that Jesus is a person. He is real! He is not some belief or being that makes us either spiritually silly or prudish and dry. He gives us living water. He refreshes and restores. He just makes sense. And His advocate, the Holy Spirit, is all about Jesus.

Paul talks about this quite a bit in his letter to the churches. In Colossians he wrote his letter in regard to this type of weird theology—a teaching without Jesus. This teaching is Gnosticism—believing in personal spiritual knowledge, an enlightenment without the foundations of sin and repentance—our salvation. Much like some of our churches today. Jesus is good, but is He enough? In Colossians, Paul makes it quite clear that *Jesus is enough!* "So then, just as you received Christ Jesus as Lord, continue to live your lives in him, rooted and built up in him, strengthened in the faith as you were taught, and overflowing with thankfulness."[25] We receive Jesus and then for many of our churches, this is the end of the road. That's it. You received Him and we forget about the roots and the buildup and the strengthening of our faith in Him and we go straight to the "Well, now what?" And the problem is that we as believers begin forgetting just how powerful Jesus is and start trying to appeal to what we think is exciting

---

[25] Colossians 2:6 (NIV).

and powerful and elevating (and it happens to our church leaders too). Jesus is enough. Jesus is exciting enough. Jesus is powerful enough. Jesus is elevating enough. Jesus is more than enough! When we begin to appeal to our senses and feelings rather than truth, the result ends up being a church filled with pride, arrogance, and a silly spirit—not the Holy One. As a result, many sincere Christians or people seeking truth and salvation walk away from church empty, confused, disappointed, and disillusioned.

Jim Cymbala in his book *Fresh Wind, Fresh Fire,* references 2 Corinthians 3:6. "The letter kills, but the Spirit gives life." He continues. "If the Holy Spirit is not given an opening among us, if his work is not welcomed, if we are afraid of what he might do, we leave ourselves nothing but death. Granted, extremists have done fanatical things in the name of the Holy Spirit that have frightened many sincere Christians away. Chaotic meetings with silly things going on and a lack of reverence for God have driven many to prefer a quiet, orderly lecture. But this is just another tactic of the enemy ... *Satan's tendency is always to push us toward one extreme or the other: deadness or fanaticism.*"[26]

"See to it that no one takes you captive through hollow and deceptive philosophy, which depends on human tradition and the elementary spiritual forces of this world

---

[26] Italics are mine because Cymbala's words are so good! He is a much better writer. Read *Fresh Wind, Fresh Fire!* This book changed my stinkin' thinkin'.

rather than on Christ."[27] Unfortunately, many of our church leaders have fallen into this trap as well. For some reason, Jesus just isn't enough. So we fill our services with elevated words and emotions instead of a *real* relationship with the Savior. Our churches have become consumed with human tradition and the need for "something" fanatic in order to grow the congregation rather than seeking Christ first and becoming the unblemished bride full of love, awe, peace, and contentment because God made us alive in Christ. He forgave us, canceled our debts, and displayed His bride unblemished because He paid it all.[28]

I have too often heard a fellow believer say something like "Wow. I just need a word from Pastor _____," "Did you hear what Pastor _____ spoke over me?" or "Pastor _____ said ..." And I have found myself in those places as well while sitting in another "prophetic" or "healing" service waiting eagerly for leadership to call me out, to say my name, to call me forward with a *word*. The problem isn't the pastor, the people, or the service. The problem is the heart and intentionality of the matter. God's word has roughly 700,000 to 800,000 words in it depending upon the translation. That equates to an easy 3 million characters within the word. There is nothing man can say to me that God has not already published. I have had men and women of God speak over me words of truth and wisdom that only

---

[27] Colossians 2:8 (NIV).

[28] Colossians 2:9–15 (NIV). We have spiritual fullness in Christ. These verses emphasize this truth!

God could have directed them to share with me; however, I do exactly what the word then tells me to do, "but test everything that is said. Hold on to what is good."[29] I have also witnessed people speak out of turn not within the realm of God's word that has misled and misguided people into confusion or a wanton desire to hear more of what that man or woman is sharing with them instead of God or witnessed a pastor pray and speak over someone who then falls in love with the charismatic pastor instead of God, the One who wants to set them free and Jesus, who is *always* enough.

Many years ago, when I came to know Jesus as my Savior and was seeking a deeper relationship with Him, I found myself seeking man's words rather than reading God's words. I often thirsted for what my pastor had to say to me to build me up or encourage my walk rather than being in God's word. I wasn't putting the time aside to get with the Father, to ask Him what the plan was, to seek, knock, and find.[30] The encouragement was that the pastor was sharing godly love, wisdom, and truth. The problem is that I was putting all my trust in man. Eventually, God led my family away from that church to a church *I did not* want to attend. In all my westernized consumerist mentality, my only argument was that this church was a megachurch for our area, but a mega "spiritually lame" church. My husband

---

[29] 1 Thessalonians 5:21 (NIV).

[30] Matthew 7:7–12.

insisted we go, so begrudgingly, I agreed. Several months into this new church, they were offering a class to figure out where you belonged in the church. My husband and I decided to attend.

During that class, the Holy Spirit did something profound in me and scales fell from my eyes.[31] I realized that it was not God whom I had been serving; it had been my beloved former pastors. God had called me away from the church I loved because I had forgotten my first love: my Abba, my Father, my God. He made me realize and understand that the pastors weren't my issue; it was my heart. My heart needed to be recalibrated back to the Father. There was no comparing the two churches because both were serving the same Jesus; there is only one. It was a matter of where God wanted me so He could bring me to where He needed me to be then, after, and now. Many things transpired from that difficult move, and through that, we experienced other parts of the hurt church, a broken system, and people who move without God. God gave us an outreach ministry, church from home, and eventually led us back to a church building with a church family, and into a pastoral role. It was everything we experienced that helped my precious family get realigned to the Father: His purpose. His words. His truths. There were people who spoke words of life and wisdom as we traveled to this place, and for a long

---

[31] Acts 9:18 (NIV). I love it when God brings an awesome and much-needed realization to bring you *fully* to Him.

time, their words and actions took merit and precedence over God's, but just like a good Father always does, His gentle discipline brought our hearts back to repentance and then peace. And that wisdom, that truth, and His spirit are never of the silly kind.

Chapter SEVEN

But Jesus Went to the Mount of Olives.

At dawn he appeared again in sat down to teach them. The teachers of the law and the Pharisees brought in a woman caught in adultery. They made her stand before the group and said to Jesus, "Teacher, this woman was caught in the act of adultery. In the Law Moses commanded us to stone such women. Now what do you say?" They were using this question at the temple courts, where all the people gathered around him, as a trap, in order to have a basis for accusing him.

But Jesus bent down and started to write on the ground with his finger. When they kept on questioning him, he straightened up and said to them, "Let any one of you who is without sin be the first to throw a stone at her." Again he stooped down and wrote on the ground.

At this, those who heard began to go away one at a time, the older ones first, until only Jesus was left, with the woman still standing there. Jesus straightened up and asked her, "Woman, where are they? Has no one condemned you?"

"No one, sir," she said. "Then neither do I condemn you," Jesus declared. "Go now and leave your life of sin."

—John 7:53–8:1–11

I find it interesting that this particular section of scripture is omitted from the earliest manuscripts of God's word. There are many theologians and scholars who have various reasons for this omission and some even argue (still today) whether or not this section should be included in the Bible. Part of the reason for the omission was the fear that women would find their adultery forgivable and therefore there would be an influx in adultery among women. Because of man's fear and lack of forgiveness and grace, a story of forgiveness was omitted from multiple Bible translations. As the church, we want to see and be the change, but only on our terms instead of only through the terms of Jesus.

Jesus did not show partiality.

Jesus drew the line in the dirt.

Jesus said if you are without sin, cast the first stone.

No stones were thrown.

Jesus doesn't fear the sin; He frees the sinner. Two thousand years ago was not much different from today: quick to omit who Jesus was and is and is to come—the forgiver of sins. Jesus built a relationship with an adulterous woman that day. This relationship altered everything. It altered her life. It altered her family's life. It altered the town. Jesus *only*. With Jesus *only*, we draw the line in the sand. We draw the line in the sand concerning sin and grievances and side with the forgiving power of Jesus. In all the hurt, pain, sorrow, and conviction, we fully and completely choose the side with Jesus. In all the differences and theologies, we side with Jesus. In all the churches, big and small, we side with Jesus. Jesus *only*.

When you're focused on Jesus *only*, then the scales fall from your eyes. Jesus *only* means there is no time for lack of unity within our church body because we operate like the body of Christ. We don't lack relational living because we relate to the sinner and the saint. We relate to the greatest and least of these. We value every member (sin and all) and intentionally live out a life worthy of the life He gave seeking to instill this unconditional, reckless love to others.

The root of relational living is Jesus. The most important relationship to building all other relationships is the one you have with your good, *good* Father and His awesome Son, Jesus. Just like the adulterous woman, this relationship changes everything you know and understand about relationships when you look at relationships through the lens of Christ's mercy and grace.

I really started to think about this omitted story and the woman at the well in late 2020. Honestly, I had been familiar with the woman at the well but never really took time to study or spend significant time getting to know her, her story, and her life-altering, relationship-transforming encounter. And just as God usually does when He is trying to get our attention, every time I thought I forgot about it, this story just kept on coming back to me and I felt a tugging to go back to it. I actually even mentioned it to a few people but didn't do anything with it. And then in the fall of 2021, I heard a song that started to bring what God was doing into light, "The Woman at the Well" by Olivia Lane.

And then it hit me. I had literally watched this story come to life in 2020. In 2020, I had the opportunity and privilege to walk alongside my mum as she fought small cell lung cancer (SCLC) to the bittersweet end. And I say bittersweet because it was bitter in so far that we lost our momma, but sweet because it was through SCLC that my mom made it to the greatest love of her life, the greatest, most awesome relationship she had always desired, and a relationship that transformed all others. And that was her relationship with the love of her life, Jesus.

The Samaritan's story is a life-giving, relationship-transforming story of God's grace and redemption. It is not just a story about a Samaritan woman but any human desperate for a satisfying life and unending grace, who is seeking love and acceptance despite past mistakes. This story is one about a Samaritan woman, my mom, me, humankind—all of us really. This story is whole life transformation, and only Jesus can do that.

> Now he had to go through Samaria. So he came to a town in Samaria called Sychar, near the plot of ground Jacob had given to his son Joseph. Jacob's well was there, and Jesus, tired as he was from the journey, sat down by the well. It was about noon.
>
> When a Samaritan woman came to draw water, Jesus said to her, "Will you give me a drink?" (His disciples had gone into the town to buy food.)
>
> The Samaritan woman said to him, "You are a Jew and I am a Samaritan woman. How can you ask me for a drink?" (For Jews do not associate with Samaritans.)
>
> Jesus answered her, "If you knew the gift of God and who it is that asks you for a drink, you would have asked him and he would have given you living water."

"Sir," the woman said, "you have nothing to draw with and the well is deep. Where can you get this living water? Are you greater than our father Jacob, who gave us the well and drank from it himself, as did also his sons and his livestock?"

Jesus answered, "Everyone who drinks this water will be thirsty again, but whoever drinks the water I give them will never thirst. Indeed, the water I give them will become in them a spring of water welling up to eternal life."

The woman said to him, "Sir, give me this water so that I won't get thirsty and have to keep coming here to draw water."[32]

My Jesus, your Jesus, this Samaritan woman's Jesus, my mom's Jesus—He was a rule breaker and relationship maker! Samaritans were not people Jews spoke to, and conversations with women were off limits. Women had no place and little respect, yet right here we see Jesus not only speaking to a Samaritan, but also a woman, and also *alone*. This would become the talk of the town. But isn't that what and where Jesus should be: the talk of our relationships, the talk of our town, and not within four walls of a building

---

[32] John 4:4–15 (NIV).

only on a designated day? This gossip shouldn't remain as a secret but should be shouted from every rooftop: this Jesus changed my life, my forever, my eternity!

I can't help but picture this Samaritan woman a lot like my own momma—full of sass,[33] a hardened heart, and no time for games. This Samaritan woman had been through it. Relationships were null and void and served one purpose, and she most likely didn't have many female friends given her history; she didn't even have a relationship to transform.

So it was with my own mom. She had a rough life and made tough choices. At the end of the day, my mom knew she had her own back. And those choices, consequences, life choices made her heart hardened and made her tougher than any woman I have ever met or will meet. She didn't need a man, and that's how she raised her four illegitimate daughters. When she wanted water, she went to the well on her own time, in her own way, and for her.

The woman at the well met the Savior during the unlikeliest of times during high noon in a difficult season of life. That day, she met the one who would satisfy not only her thirst but her soul because you can't meet a spiritual need with a physical thing, and the only man who knew that was Jesus. The only friend who knew that was Jesus. The only relationship that would matter and transform all

---

[33] Maybe a little less colorful words due to the lack of language available to the Samaritan woman—but still.

others—Jesus—was the only one who knew the spiritual need would transform all others!

And in verse 13, Jesus reveals that *only* through Him do we gain eternal life. Yet the Samaritan woman continues to fight it. To her and so many, this is just another man, another relationship, another physical need with its own wants, desires, and motives. But Jesus, in verse 16, does what only He can do in full love and discipline; He calls her bluff. He tells her to call her husband and come back *knowing* that she has no husband but has had many and is currently with another man. He does not do this to shame her but to bring her healing. He doesn't close the doors because of her sin. He opens the doors of healing and forgiveness for herself. This truth revealed His truth and that He *alone* is the source of making us into the unblemished bride He calls us to be. He brings all things from the darkness to the light to set us free.[34]

A spiritual need cannot be met with a physical thing (man, house, car, kids, clothes, social media) or a counterfeit thing, if you will; a cylinder doesn't fit into a square peg. My mom, my sisters, all of us wanted the physical thing; we wanted the healing, but that wasn't what she needed. She needed what I had spent seventeen years praying for: a relationship with the Savior. She needed the *spiritual* healing. And just like the Samaritan woman, my mom

---

[34] Ephesians 5:13 (NIV). Don't let the enemy hide your sin. He's the dirty one, not you.

needed Jesus to reveal Himself not in the physical want but in the spiritual *need*. My mom's desires for everything else to make her happy or to make her fulfilled or to cover the pain and the loss that she carried for the better part of forty years couldn't come in the physical. The filling, healing, and love were *only* going to come from the spiritual. And that came in the form of small cell lung cancer. My God, my good, *good* Father knew the daughter He made.

A well-intentioned pastor prayed for my mom one Sunday morning. And he, with all good motivation and intention, wanted to pray that cancer right out of her as many well-intended pastors do. At the end of his prayer, with honor and respect, I told the pastor that she had already been healed. Rather than stop and listen and accept that God does what He does and heals how He sees fit, this pastor looked at me with unbelief. He couldn't accept that. He couldn't accept that there are just things of the Spirit we will never understand, and we cannot force His hand to do anything but His will. I have watched people walk away from the church and the love of Christ because of this lack of understanding. God is God. We are not. His ways are not our ways, but I trust in Him anyway. What if instead of placing our demands on Him, we just loved Him, loved others, and met people at their needs, inviting them to put their stones away, draw the line in the sand, and live in freedom from sin?

The Savior had already been before her, but the Samaritan woman couldn't see because she was blind to him by her hurt, pain, and bad choices. She believed she was unworthy, knew the Messiah would come, but would He see her in the midst of her sin, her adultery, and her multiple husbands? Yes, in fact, He revealed Himself so powerfully to her in love and discipline that she suddenly couldn't wait to tell people about the Savior of the world—the one who didn't meet her physical wants but the One who has given her living water, the One who covered and healed her very soul. He saw her! Imagine if, as a church, we stopped and just saw the person as Jesus does: a beautiful disaster.

And then we know something extraordinary takes place that day at the well and that the testimony she gave to the town was wildly impactful because the following verses and verse 39 say that many Samaritans (the Samaritans, the castaways, the less than worthy) from the town came to believe in Him because of this woman's testimony.

She couldn't wait to tell people about the *real* relationship in her life. The *real* man in her life. The *real* friend in her life.

This same thing happened for my mom. I believe that when my mom faced her diagnosis and the doctor said she had from two weeks to two months to live in February 2020 without doing chemo, I believe that the Savior was already before her saying, "I am He. Here I am. Look up, Becky. See Me." It was that day, on her high noon, that she finally took her eyes off the brokenness and the broken relationships and looked up—eyes on Jesus. How do I know that? Because

I know that our God is a God of impeccable timing and the One who mends and heals even the most shattered of people. I believe that if this disease would have happened at any other time, my mom would have fallen into even more bitterness. I believe she would have been even angrier and would have thrown even more anger out of her little five-foot, two-inch frame. But God knew it was time. He knew that it was only the spiritual healing that would tear down that thick, tall wall, bring her a healing beyond this life, and get her to the kingdom and to a life that had purpose beyond what she ever imagined in her short seventy-two years.

Over the course of the remaining nine months, I would watch and listen to my mom have more gratitude in her heart than I had ever seen. I would watch her thank and exude patience in situations where I would have expected to see her former self, "the Intimidator." She would literally tell doctors and nurses of God's grace and goodness. She would tell another cancer patient struggling during radiation how good God is and to remember that. I would listen to her tell one of my former students (now a nurse) how good God is and to remember that "God loves you, honey girl." And after we left that day, after nine days of radiation on her brain to give us just a couple more months, Boogs would take my hand in the car and say, "You know, honey girl, I struggled to find love my whole life. I just wanted loved. And here, I had that love—the love of my life—the whole time." I would have the privilege to baptize her at her home with my niece and her husband because my momma (on that beautiful, God-ordained, perfect day) had always wanted to be baptized. It was the best and right thing to do.

On the day she passed away in October of 2020, I would have the greatest gift yet (as if my mom's entire relationship transformation with the Savior wasn't enough) to lay at her feet and have God give me the clearest vision I had ever seen. As she took her last breath, I saw her curled around the feet of her Savior as I lay wrapped around my momma's own delicate feet. The woman who had ushered me into life, I now had the privilege of ushering into the other side of eternity.

Just like the Samaritan woman, my mom's testimony and story has changed lives because she started living loved. She started living with her relationship with Jesus first, and that changed everything and every relationship she had. The heart softened, the hugs deepened, and the love overflowed. Her eyes were opened the day she met the Savior, just like the Samaritan woman. Her search was over. She found the love of her life: her living water. She became a part of his beautiful bride.

Followers of Christ, I am really just tattling on myself when I say that I was the one willing to cast the first stone at my momma. I wanted to point out the splinter in her eye when I had a gigantic plank hanging out of my own.[35] In my lame attempts to bring her to Jesus, I missed out on

---

[35] Matthew 7:3–5 (NIV).

the most important part of salvation: love. I failed to see her at the well. I failed to see her as Jesus saw her. I failed. Just like the well-intended pastor that Sunday morning, I failed to love her right where she was and neglected to see God working all things out for His glory. And bride of Christ, that will be where we remain if we don't start living loved by the Savior of the world. I wanted to get my mom to church by the recognition of her sins rather than watch her flourish through a relationship with Jesus and His love, grace, mercy and living water. It is time to become the church—*the bride*—as God intended.

Chapter EIGHT

A Unified Church, a Beautiful Bride

As I finish this book, review these pages, and reflect on its purpose, God's purpose for my life, and God's good and perfect plan, so many things have changed since this first began. When this book began to form in the deepest recesses of my heart and the inner womb of my spirit, I had no idea that God was really working on my own convictions and shortcomings and placing a desire to love people—*all people*—more deeply, more freely, and without constraint (including myself). For way too long, I allowed the church—not the authentic bride of Christ, not Jesus—define who I was and my actions and my motives. I knew Jesus, but I wasn't allowing His freedom and grace to wash over me and every relationship and experience the true undignified reckless love of the Father. And if we're being honest with ourselves (pastors, leaders, churchgoers, Chreasters—yes, you too) we live a vast majority of our life attempting to please our way to heaven. In the pleasing, we judge the people who don't come to church and the ones who show up every Sunday. We assume the worst about the least of these and the best of these and their motives and hearts. We cast stones without restraint. Even now, as I finish the remaining pages of my heart's desires, I look at a "Welcome to Our Neighborhood" cake that a neighbor delivered this afternoon. This cake wasn't delivered by the righteous neighbor on the street. This cake was delivered by an addict's grandmother, by the brokenhearted—the one God is closest to. That neighbor was encouragement on that particular day. That neighbor sought to lift us up when the cards were down. That neighbor unified with Christ today. Do I know if that neighbor knows Jesus as her Lord and Savior? Not yet. But I plan on finding out through building community with her, intentionally seeking a relationship with her, and demonstrating God's good and perfect love for her through conversations and dessert.

On the other hand, as our smaller chunk of the church body performed baptisms one particular Sunday and another larger chunk of the church body did as well, I couldn't help but notice that some of the people from church were not quite as "neighborly" as I would have hoped. We were met with awkwardness and a competitive spirit. I desired for these two churches to blend that morning, share in worship and baptisms, and be the bride. My smiles and "This is awesome" weren't enough that morning. Rather than listen to the Spirit telling me to break the mold, approach the leadership, and unite as one, I was consumed with the "unneighborly" and fear of rejection from man. What would our leadership say? How would our worship leader feel? Would he be able to play with them? What about the message? What if the congregation didn't want to join with another church on "our" special Sunday? I allowed my desire for man's approval and fear of rejection to consume my heart rather than listen to the conviction from the Holy Spirit to stand in unity as the bride—whether they or we liked it or not.

There's a reason God's good, holy, and perfect word speaks so much concerning our hearts, how we love others, and our treatment of others. He knew we would be perfectly imperfect messes. He knew we would need the constant reminders as His body to unify, reunite, and strengthen in our solitude. God doesn't need us to play church. He desires us to be His church and to become the bride His Son so desperately desired that He gave his life for us. Sometimes, I think we forget that. Sometimes, I think we hear that over and over, but it loses its power, its meaning. When we stop, hit our knees, open our arms wide, and look up, I pray we remember all that He has done to unify us as one. When our eyes are fixated on the Father, what else is even worthy to steal our focus away?

Church, it is time. It is time to rise up and be chain

breakers over our church and its systems. It is time to live out the life of Christ every day in our walk, in our talk, in our minds, and in our hearts. It is time to live the life that was freely given. Let's stop comparing, staring, finger-pointing, and worrying about "stealing" church members (or shutting our doors) and get our eyes on the Father. Let's stop church shopping and hopping and fix what's right in front of us with God's holy word leading the way. No more fads or movements. Just us and Him united in a beautiful relationship with all people regardless of the cloth or fabric that has been woven into their lives.

Church, let's live loved.

Afterword

The heavens declare the glory of God;
the skies proclaim the work of his hands.
Day after day they pour forth speech;
night after night they reveal knowledge.
They have no speech, they use no words;
no sound is heard from them.
Yet their voice goes out into all the earth,
their words to the ends of the world.
In the heavens God has pitched a tent for the sun.
It is like a bridegroom coming out of his chamber,
like a champion rejoicing to run his course.
It rises at one end of the heavens
and makes its circuit to the other;
nothing is deprived of its warmth.
The law of the LORD is perfect,
refreshing the soul.
The statutes of the LORD are trustworthy,
making wise the simple.

The precepts of the Lord are right,
giving joy to the heart.
The commands of the Lord are radiant,
giving light to the eyes.
The fear of the Lord is pure,
enduring forever.
The decrees of the Lord are firm,
and all of them are righteous.
They are more precious than gold,
than much pure gold;
they are sweeter than honey,
than honey from the honeycomb.
By them your servant is warned;
in keeping them there is great reward.
But who can discern their own errors?
Forgive my hidden faults.
Keep your servant also from willful sins;
may they not rule over me.
Then I will be blameless,
innocent of great transgression.
May these words of my mouth and
this meditation of my heart
be pleasing in your sight,
Lord, my Rock and my Redeemer.

Psalm 19 is written by David, a man after God's own heart. David was not sinless, but he was found blameless and this was the constant meditation of his heart: to strive to be holy as God is holy. David was consumed with the Spirit of God. He wanted to be anointed by God with the power of the Holy Spirit so he could *do* the word of God (not just hear it) and then serve Him all of his days in all of God's ways. He knew that living in the Holy Spirit would empower him to live in daily victories over struggles, hurt, pain, envy, sin, his darkest moments—*everything*. And then, by living in that power, David knew he could channel that love to everyone, including Saul, the man who would try to kill David most of his days. David wasn't consumed with "church" or churched living; David was consumed by kingdom and kingdom living.

In Psalm 19, we see this man after God's own heart in complete awe of the heavens. He is enthralled by the sheer beauty of the world around him. His descriptions of the earth and all that is in it are powerful and inspiring. He comments that the heavens and the sky use no voice yet their praises spill forth to the ends of the earth. To put it simply, their actions speak louder than their words. They need no building or constraint. They do not need to be told how or when to praise; the earth just does it. They are not consumed by who is watching or how many see them; they just praise any way. They praise when we are awake and when we sleep. They praise in every calm and every storm to the ends of the earth. The skies and heavens cry to the glory of God always.

This then is the prayer of David's heart: that this would

be the words from his mouth and the meditation of his heart.

Friends, I pray this for us too, and may the bride of Christ be forever changed to shine for His glory and His glory alone.

CPSIA information can be obtained
at www.ICGtesting.com
Printed in the USA
BVHW041428010623
665226BV00006B/319